Faith

Hope

Love

Faith
Hope
Love

A 28-Day Journey

Zach Maddox

REDEFINING
Faith
RESOURCES

Faith Hope Love

Published by Redefining Faith Resources

ISBN: 978-0-98900-270-7
eISBN: 978-0-98900-271-4
pdfISBN: 978-0-98900-272-1

DEDICATION

Thank you Lord for a faith, hope and love that lasts from now to
eternity.

To my best friend and wife, Shellie, you have challenged me to
have a great faith in God, a profound hope in the future, and a
deep love of life in Jesus.

CONTENTS

ACKNOWLEDGMENTS

To my wife, Shellie - you are the love of my life. To my kids, Nathaniel, Haley, and Lucas, I love being your dad.

To my grandmother, Lorraine Darling, you have lived out your faith for many years.

To my dad, Bob Maddox, you showed me how to live out faith and abide in Jesus. I cannot thank you enough for the countless hours you spent reviewing these devotional entries and editing my text.

To my mom, Brenda Maddox, you selflessly served at home to raise me, along with my three siblings, to love God.

To my in-laws, Steve and JoAnn Lewis, you raised a godly daughter and continue to encourage others in the faith.

To my siblings, Nikole, Nan, and Stephen, and their families, you have kept the faith and continue to advance the Kingdom.

To our best friends, Aaron and Heather Santmyire, you continue to challenge us and inspire us to take the message of Jesus around the world.

To Dr. Mike and Darla Rakes, you are great spiritual mentors and passionate pursuers of God.

To Bernhard, Erene, Shane, Mandy, Jon, Cheri, Jim, Liz, Adam, Melissa, Rob, Evangeline, and the many others who prayed for this devotional.

To Jason, Aaron, and the Prodigy Pixel team for their work on the cover.

To Joel for his creative and innovative work on the Holy Land stop motion film.

To our co-laborers around the world who desire to see God's glory fill the whole earth. You inspire us all.

FOREWORD

All journeys have mountains and valleys, deserts and springs, atmospheres and climates. Zach Maddox is a great one to guide you along the way. Zach has seen and experienced almost every climate in the world and knows first hand the joys and dangers of being a follower of Jesus. He has been committed to carrying the good news personally all over the world.

Zach has a passion for life, family and has integrated his faith into the deeper parts of his being. He lives bold and unafraid and happy to sacrifice if it means someone is helped along the way. He encourages people to discover for themselves that God is their friend.

John 15:15 I do not call you slaves anymore, because a slave doesn't know what his master is doing. I have called you friends, because I have made known to you everything I have heard from My Father.

In this little book Zach helps you shift the way you think about your relationship with God. He delivers a message of understanding and clarity about the things you'll need on this journey. He brings home powerfully the message that all God's communication to you originates from love. That personal love is what impacts the heart so strongly and initiates a response not a sense of religious duty. If you'll follow Zach's direction love will become the language and trajectory of your heart.

Whether you're an experienced spiritual traveler or new to the idea of pursuing God this little book will help you survive your lowest valleys and enjoy the view from the higher places.

Blessings,

Dr. Mike Rakes

Lead Pastor, Winston Salem First

PREFACE

Faith, Hope, and Love... virtues describing life in Jesus. They define our family's journey in pursuit of the living God. "Day 1" explains how Shellie and I have been blessed by these three life-changing attributes. My desire is to inspire you to live a meaningful faith-filled life. My prayer is for this devotional to help you in the journey.

Followers of Jesus gain by reading Scripture, responding to and praying over it. Although this devotional is not Scripture, ask God to speak to your heart about the content. Pick up a journal and respond to each entry. You can also go online and visit my website journal at zachmaddox/faithjournal. I would count it a privilege to dialogue with you there.

Take the necessary time to read and absorb this 28-day journey. In the course of the next several weeks have a "burning bush" experience with God, where He confronts any possible unbelief and leads you into a more intimate walk with Him. May you find yourself a transformed person a month from now, someone who has redefined their faith.

Zach

DAY 1
BLESSED TO BE A BLESSING

"and I will bless you and make your name great, so that you will be a blessing"
Genesis 12:2

The Role of God's Children

A common thread throughout the Bible is God's people being blessed to be a blessing. The covenant with Abraham was, *"and I will bless you and make your name great, so that you will be a blessing" (Genesis 12:2)*. God intended Abraham's descendants to bless the nations.

The Call

Psalm 67:1 reads, *"May God be gracious to us and bless us and make his face to shine upon us, that your way may be known on earth, your saving power among all nations."* Not only have God's people been blessed to be a blessing, but they are blessed as they respond to His divine purpose for their lives.

Faith, Hope, and Love

Shellie and I have found this to be especially true in our lives. We have seen tremendous blessings according to the three Christian virtues of faith, hope, and love.

Encountering Hardships

As Shellie and I attempt to bless others we are blessed. We have experienced a tremendous growth in faith. When living in Sudan we faced numerous challenges. We encountered daily hardships in an oppressive society, was confined for a day at a police station following a car accident, rebels from Darfur fought government troops across the Nile River from our home, experienced demonstrations in Kenya, and vacated Madagascar during a government overthrow while visiting friends to relieve stress. When we returned to the States we were exhausted.

The Blessing of Faith

In the U.S. we gave extra time to reading the Bible, praying and singing songs of worship. We began to realize our hardships had developed a profound faith in an omniscient God. We better understood James 1:2-3, *"Count it all joy, my brothers, when you meet trials of various kinds, for you know that the testing of your faith produces steadfastness."* Adversity is uncomfortable but is a blessing when viewed from a right perspective. Faith is the greatest of all blessings. The next two blessings grow out of the blessing of faith.

The Blessing of Hope

When Shellie and I decided to pursue overseas work we were public school teachers in the Chicago area. One reason for not serving in the Middle East was college loans. Seeking to pursue God's heart for the nations, we made applications for international work. We put our house on the market. In six days we had a contract on the place. Twenty-five days later the sale was complete. The education loans were paid and we were able to fulfill our desire to work overseas.

Returning from Sudan our family went for a dental check-up. The bill came to $786. Four months later we received a gift in the amount of $790. A pastor friend says our walk with the Lord should be constantly amazing but never surprising. We were amazed the check had been sent but not surprised because of our great God.

The Blessing of Love

After a few years of marriage, we learned medical intervention was needed to have children. After a prolonged period and miscarriage Shellie became pregnant with Nathaniel. His name means "gift of God."

While living in Sudan Shellie used fertility medicine once again but to no avail. We decided to simply trust God. Within six months she was pregnant with Haley. Her name means "unexpected gift".

In the fall of 2012 we welcomed the latest addition to the family, Lucas. His name means "bringer of light." In six years we have been blessed with children and, most of all, with the light of an unfolding faith journey. What doctors thought impossible without medicine, God made possible.

The Challenge

God desires to bless you while being a blessing to the nations. Participate in what God is doing by praying, giving, and even going.

"God help me to be a blessing to the nations. Give me wisdom and strength to use my time, talents, and resources for the advancement of your kingdom."

In what ways can you intentionally bless others? I encourage you to respond in a personal journal or share your comments online at zachmaddox.com/faithjournal.

_____

_____

_____

_____

_____

_____

_____

_____

_____

_____

_____

_____

_____

_____

_____

_____

I also encourage you to visit zachmaddox.com and select the "podcast" button for a free podcast message of this content in iTunes.

PART 1

FAITH

"Faith is the confidence that what we hope for will actually happen; it gives us assurance about things we cannot see."

Hebrews 11:1 – NLT

DAY 2
FROM ROUTINE TO RADICAL

"Did not our hearts burn within us while he talked to us on the road, while he opened to us the Scriptures?" Luke 24:32

How God Can Transform Your Life

In the spring of 2006, my wife and I resigned our teaching jobs in the Chicago area, sold our home and furnishings, and crossed the Atlantic with our one-year-old son to work in an international school in Khartoum, Sudan. We moved from *routine* to *radical*.

From Head to Heart

While residing in Sudan Jesus began to reveal Himself in an overwhelming way. By facing adversity in a challenging environment we spent extravagant time reading the Bible, praying, and worshipping. Our life in Jesus shifted from a mind to heart experience.

Carl Meadearis in his book *Speaking of Jesus: The Art of Not-Evangelism* wrote, "The kingdom of Jesus has somehow become a religion of the mind rather than a spiritual response of the heart. We focus on psychological compliance rather than spiritual dependence upon the teachings of Jesus and the guidance of the Comforter, the Holy Spirit." [1]

We experienced Jesus in profound ways as we engaged in His plan and spent time in His Word. One of my favorite Scriptures is from Luke 24:32. Jesus leaves the men on the Emmaus road and they say to each other, *"Did not our hearts burn within us while he talked to us on the road, while he opened to us the Scriptures?"* These two travelers say it best; Jesus can captivate the heart in radical ways, when given the right opportunity.

We removed ourselves from comfortable surroundings and gained a better awareness of Jesus. Our hearts began to burn "within us" and Scripture became alive.

Francis Chan in his book *Crazy Love* had a similar experience and gave a greater heart response to the gospel; a crazy love for God. He wrote, "Until just a few years ago I was quite happy with how God was working in me and in the church. Then God began changing my heart." He wrote this happened through Scripture reading and third world country experiences. [2]

The Goal

This devotional is created to bring you closer to Jesus. I hope to challenge, inspire, and inform you of how to fulfill the purpose of God. My hope is for Jesus to move you into a passionate pursuit of Him and His plan.

Oswald Chambers in his devotional, *My Utmost for His Highest* wrote, "Being saved and seeing Jesus is not the same thing. Many are partakers of God's grace who have never seen Jesus. When once you have seen Jesus, you can never be the same; other things do not appeal as they used to do." [3]

The Challenge

May you see Jesus, move out of a routine type of life, and experience Him in radical ways.

"God, may you burn within my heart. Open my mind to scripture. Move me from an ordinary faith to an extraordinary faith."

In what ways have you seen Jesus in your life? How has scripture burned within you? I encourage you to respond in a personal journal or share your comments online at zachmaddox.com/faithjournal.

_____

_____

_____

_____

_____

_____

1 - Copyright 2011 Carl Medearis. *Speaking of Jesus* published by David C Cook. Publisher permission required to reproduce. All rights reserved.

2 - Copyright 2008 Francis Chan. *Crazy Love* published by David C Cook. Publisher permission required to reproduce. All rights reserved.

3 - Taken from *My Utmost for His Highest* by Oswald Chambers, edited by James Reimann, © 1992 by Oswald Chambers Publications Assn., Ltd., and used by permission of Discovery House Publishers, Grand Rapids MI 49501. All rights reserved.

DAY 3
TO S/HELL AND BACK

"They came to the other side of the sea..." Mark 5:1

The Power of God Revealed in a Storm

We spent 4 months "camping out" in our house in Sudan; sleeping on air mattresses, using a single knife, pot and pan, borrowing a table and chairs from friends. Our container had not yet arrived. We were dealing daily with intense heat (around 115 degrees) and trying to learn Arabic to simply buy food.

While traveling home from a meeting in Khartoum I drove past a Shell station. I thought to myself, "If they just drop the 'S' from the sign, they would have it right." I felt like we were experiencing the worst place known to man.

A Storm on Galilee

Mark chapter 4:35-41 records a story of Jesus crossing the sea of Galilee with his disciples and encountering a storm. Did Jesus know the storm was coming? Did He actually lead the disciples into a storm? What does this say about Him? Does this reveal that Jesus desires to make Himself known more than make our lives comfortable?

Jesus spoke to the multitudes, separated his disciples from the crowd and directed them to cross to the other side. While the disciples are crossing the sea a violent storm threatened their lives but for a reason. They were going to gain a greater awareness of Jesus' divine nature. In the midst of the storm the disciples pursued Jesus and the sea became calm.

The Lord faithfully points believers in the direction they should go. Do you listen? God sometimes separates His followers in order to reveal the fullness of His nature. In the midst of life's storm He often reveals His supernatural power.

Are you presently facing adversity? Are you looking to Jesus for help?

Who Can Calm a Storm?

After the sea became calm, the disciples asked, *"Who then is this, that even the wind and the sea obey him?" (Mark 4:41)* The friend and teacher Jesus was not being revealed but rather the Son of God. The disciples regularly listened to His teachings but this storm revealed who He is. He spoke and creation responded.

The greatest part of the story happens in chapter 5:1, *"They came to the other side of the sea."* Jesus instructed His disciples, "Let us go across to the other side". They faced a storm between the two shores but Jesus kept his promise; they crossed to the other side.

The Challenge

When facing life's storms, pursue Jesus! He will make Himself powerfully known to you. As Jesus brought my family and I through our storm in Sudan, He will bring you to the other side of your storm.

"God, as I face hardships, may I hold onto the promise that you will bring me through to the other side. Give me a steadfast spirit to endure so that I might see you more clearly."

What kinds of challenges are you facing right now? In what ways have you seen God powerfully work through adversity in your past? I encourage you to respond in a personal journal or share your comments online at zachmaddox.com/faithjournal.

_____

_____

_____

_____

_____

_____

_____

_____

_____

I encourage you to visit vimeo.com/zachmaddox/unveiling-jesus for an onsite video bible teaching captured from the shores of Galilee.

DAY 4
REDEFINING FAITH

"So you see, faith by itself isn't enough. Unless it produces good deeds, it is dead and useless" James 2:17 - NLT

A Lifestyle of Sharing Jesus

In my opinion some of the scariest verses in the Bible are Matthew 7:22-23, *"On judgment day many will say to me, 'Lord! Lord! We prophesied in your name and cast out demons in your name and performed many miracles in your name.' But I will reply, 'I never knew you. Get away from me, you who break God's laws.'"* - NLT

Makes you think twice about your relationship with Jesus, doesn't it? These verses contributed to the "Redefining Faith" name on my website.

Faith as a Motivating Belief

One definition of faith is a "system of religious belief". Faith is important and necessary yet James takes it a step further by stating, *"So you see, faith by itself isn't enough. Unless it produces good deeds, it is dead and useless" (James 2:17)* - NLT. Genuine faith should motivate you to love God and love people; should motivate you to action.

Verse 21 declares, *"Not everyone who calls out to me, 'Lord! Lord!' will enter the Kingdom of Heaven. Only those who actually do the will of my Father in heaven will enter"* - NLT (emphasis added). Life in Jesus involves "doing."

When Zacchaeus encountered Jesus he was motivated to give half of his possessions to the poor and pay back four times as much from anything wrongful gain. Jesus declared, *"Today salvation has come to this house" (Luke 19:9)*. His actions were not necessary for salvation but they were evidence of a life changed by encountering Jesus.

Knowing Jesus

Weekly attendance at church, reading daily a chapter in the Bible, and saying grace before dinner may better represent familial habits than a genuine relationship with Jesus.

Ask yourself this question: Do your conversations about Jesus match your lifestyle? Maybe you should start with, are you telling others about Jesus at all? If you know Jesus, if you have genuinely encountered Him, you cannot help but talk about Him. The better your relationship with Jesus, the more you love people and the more you want others to have this incredible gift you have been given.

May your faith be redefined, affirmed, and amplified as you pursue Jesus. There is no better way to obey Christ's command then to "make disciples".

The Challenge

Begin today to live out a faith motivated by pure love for God, a faith that requires more than taking up space on a pew or saying a prayer before dinner, a faith that brings real meaning and hope for the future.

"God compel me to live out my faith. Fill me with a passion to be active in this world for you."

In what ways has your faith motivated you to action? What are you doing to display the love of Jesus to those you know? I encourage you to respond in a personal journal or share your comments online at zachmaddox.com/faithjournal.

_____

_____

_____

_____

_____

_____

_____

_____

_____

_____

_____

_____

_____

DAY 5
GOD OVER ALL

"What therefore you worship as unknown, this I proclaim to you." Acts 17:23

God's Desire to Set You Free

Two thousand years ago the city of Athens was a city filled with gods. They were the world's foremost collector of gods.

City of Idols

Athens had ransacked the theologies of many people around them, gathering every deity they could possibly transport to their city by cart and by ship. These idols lined both sides of the roads and covered a rocky hillside called the Acropolis, where the Parthenon had been built.

While visiting this city the Apostle Paul was grieved by the numerous idols. He engaged some of the citizens of Athens in dialogue about their Unknown God - One not contained in form.

Acts 17: 16, 22-23

"Now while Paul was waiting for them at Athens, his spirit was provoked within him as he saw that the city was full of idols.... So Paul, standing in the midst of the Areopagus, said: 'Men of Athens, I perceive that in every way you are very religious. For as I passed along and observed the objects of your worship, I found also an altar with this inscription, 'To the unknown god.' What therefore you worship as unknown, this I proclaim to you.'"

A Plague-infested City

The story surrounding the "Unknown God" goes back to a time when the city was experiencing a plague. They were sacrificing to the hundreds of idols they already worshipped but the plagued continued. Out of desperation they sent a delegation to the island of Crete to fetch a man by the name of Epimenides.

He told them that the god they angered was unknown to them and then gave them a plan to invoke his help. Part of the plan was to acknowledge their ignorance of the god's name. The plan worked. They wanted to dedicate an altar to him, but to whom? Rather than offend this god who was pleased to respond to their admission of ignorance, they named the altar "to an unknown god."

The Inflation Factor

By the time the Apostle Paul came to Athens the city had added a couple hundred more idols. Idolatry, by its very nature, has a built-in inflation factor. Once people reject the one true God in favor of lesser deities, they eventually discover that it takes an infinite number of lesser deities to fill the true God's shoes.

Paul saw Athens prostituting mankind's sacred privilege of worship upon mere wood and stone. His spirit became provoked within him.

Idols Among Us or Just Us

Although you may not see literal idols in the form of stone or wood lining your streets, idolatry still exist. The list is extensive - superstition, celebrities, money... but self-idolatry tops the charts. Too often faulty feelings, unwholesome desires, less than perfect looks, and shoddy ideas are elevated over the supremacy of God and we miss connecting with the one true Lord. The end result is a failure to find meaning and everlasting life.

Faith is about the Lord. When God becomes your total need and concern, when His intentions becomes your desire, when His way becomes your way, then life becomes holy and complete.

Place your faith in God. Only He and His blessing can bring meaning to your life.

The Challenge

God wants to set you free from a world falsely portrayed as a place of peace and safety to usher you into everlasting life. Will you choose God over self today?

"God you are my god. I want to serve you and nothing else. I ask you to set me free from selfish desires and I invite you to be enthroned in my heart."

What kinds of idols do you think exist in the world today? I encourage you to respond in a personal journal or share your comments online at zachmaddox.com/faithjournal.

_____

_____

_____

_____

_____

_____

_____

_____

_____

_____

_____

_____

_____

_____

_____

_____

I encourage you to visit vimeo.com/zachmaddox/unknown-god for an onsite video bible teaching captured from Mars Hill in Athens, Greece.

DAY 6
TOUGH EXPECTATIONS

"If anyone would come after me, let him deny himself and take up his cross daily and follow me." Luke 9:23

What Jesus Expects of His Followers

Luke 6:46, *"Why do you call me 'Lord, Lord,' and not do what I tell you?"*

No Middle Ground

Jesus is either Lord of our lives, or He is not. There really is no middle ground. Jesus doesn't make room for middle ground. In the previous verse, Jesus is telling the crowd, "Look, you can't call me Lord (Master) and not do what I say." Jesus makes this statement after He has run through a list of what He expects.

Luke 6:27-36

"But I say to you who hear, love your enemies, do good to those who hate you, bless those who curse you, pray for those who abuse you. To one who strikes you on the cheek, offer the other also, and from one who takes away

26

your cloak do not withhold your tunic either. Give to everyone who begs from you, and from one who takes away your goods do not demand them back. And as you wish that others would do to you, do so to them.

"If you love those who love you, what benefit is that to you? For even sinners love those who love them. And if you do good to those who do good to you, what benefit is that to you? For even sinners do the same. And if you lend to those from whom you expect to receive, what credit is that to you? Even sinners lend to sinners, to get back the same amount. But love your enemies, and do good, and lend, expecting nothing in return, and your reward will be great, and you will be sons of the Most High, for he is kind to the ungrateful and the evil. Be merciful, even as your Father is merciful.'"

Loving Your enemies and Other Such Nonsense

Becoming a true disciple of Jesus is tough work. It requires placing others before you. It requires dying to self. Loving an enemy is an impossible thing to do without the transforming power of Jesus at work in your life. Even when He has taken up residence in your heart, you have to be mindful to pray for those who abuse you to gain the mind of Christ.

I Thought Jesus Would Make My Life Easy

Too many people have fallen into the trap that Jesus "blesses" their life at will. They think Jesus will give them a house, a spouse, children, and trips to Disney World. If you can show me in the Bible where that is found, I can show you where it is not (Luke 9:23).

The Challenge

Find practical ways to bless those who abuse you. Be willing to buy someone lunch who does not have the ability to pay you back. Choose Jesus as Lord and then follow His leading in your life.

"Jesus I've asked you to be my Savior but have struggled to make you Lord. I want you to be Lord of my life. Lead me and I will follow."

How can you show love to those that abuse you? I encourage you to respond in a personal journal or share your comments online at zachmaddox.com/faithjournal.

_____

_____

_____

_____

_____

_____

_____

_____

_____

_____

_____

_____

_____

DAY 7
DIRECT ACCESS

"And behold, the curtain of the temple was torn in two, from top to bottom."
Matthew 27:51

The Profound Accessibility of a Living God

Dark, candle-lit hallways adorn the Church of the Holy Sepulcher, the traditional site of Jesus' death and burial in Jerusalem. My son, Nate, did not fully understand what we were visiting but he did like the candles being lit by others as they prayed.

A Shrouded Area

After seeing the location where many people believe Jesus was crucified, we went to the shrouded area marked as His burial place. The gothic edifice monitored by the Eastern Orthodox, Roman Catholic and Armenian Apostolic churches is an interesting place.

An Interior Chamber

The Aedicule, the structure built on top of Jesus' tomb, has two rooms that can hold only 4 or 5 people. We entered the first room and waited for others to be ushered out of the interior area. Nate and I entered the innermost chamber with a couple of other people. They knelt at the altar and prayed.

Access Everywhere

After we walked out Nate asked, "Dad, why didn't we pray in there?" I replied, "Because we can pray to God anywhere. There is no difference if we pray to Jesus in our home or in that small room."

"Oh, okay!" My 5-year old was satisfied with the answer.

Holy of Holies

I never cease to be amazed how God sent His Son to die on a cross that we might have direct access to Him, regardless of location.

Matthew records what happened upon Jesus' death. *"And Jesus cried out again with a loud voice and yielded up His spirit. And behold, the curtain of the temple was torn in two, from top to bottom. And the earth shook, and the rocks were split" (Mathew 27:50, 51).*

The curtain was tore in two, separating the main sanctuary from the Holy of Holies. The place was only accessible to the high priest, where he presented the needs of the people. Meaning, they could not have direct access to God.

Jesus broke down the barrier. With His death and resurrection we come directly to God. We can pray at home, in the car, or at a place dedicated to worship. All locations are equally significant because the Holy Spirit abides in you. You have become His temple.

The Challenge

Take time to consider the cost Christ paid for your access to God. Thank the Father for sending His Son. Thank Jesus for His sacrifice on the cross. Thank the Holy Spirit for filling the temple of your heart.

We should never take for granted our access to the Creator of heaven and earth. Talk to Him daily. Through Jesus you have been given a wonderful opportunity.

"Jesus, thank you for dying on the cross. Thank you for giving me unrestricted access to God. I ask you to remind me daily to spend time in your presence."

How do you take advantage of your access to God? I encourage you to respond in a personal journal or share your comments online at zachmaddox.com/faithjournal.

_____

_____

_____

_____

_____

_____

_____

_____

_____

_____

DAY 8
LIVE DEAD

"Truly, truly, I say to you, unless a grain of wheat falls into the earth and dies, it remains alone; but if it dies, it bears much fruit." John 12:24

Bringing Glory to God

We often come to Christ in prayer with an agenda. He has his own list of items and we have to decide, do we yield to His or demand our own? To die to our plans and trust God is best. Bringing glory to God requires living-dead.

John 12:24-25

"Truly, truly, I say to you, unless a grain of wheat falls into the earth and dies, it remains alone; but if it dies, it bears much fruit. Whoever loves his life loses it, and whoever hates his life in this world will keep it for eternal life."

The Triumphant Entry

Days before speaking these words to His disciples Jesus entered Jerusalem with shouts of *"Hosanna, blessed is he who comes in the name of the Lord!"*

People were hoping for an earthly ruler. They assumed He would quickly establish His kingdom.

A Different Kind of Glory

Instead Jesus tells the crowd the time has come for Him to be glorified but not in a manner they expect. Glory through death!

Jesus says, "This is how it is going to work. I am going to bless people by dying."

We Think So Differently

This did not make sense to the disciples. They thought the best thing would be for His ministry to continue. Things were finally coming together. He started out with a few and now had a multitude. Momentum was in His favor. The ministry was growing. Why die?

Death Then Life

The way of fruitfulness, however, lies through death. Unless the wheat falls into the ground and "dies" it will not bear fruit. Through death the way of fruitfulness is activated.

Trusting God

Shorty after moving to Jerusalem our kids began to experience difficulties. The worst was our daughter experiencing spiking fevers, causing febrile seizures. I watched our beautiful 2-year old seizing on the floor one morning and heard God speak to my heart, "Can you trust me with your daughter? Can you trust me with your kids, your wife, your entire life?"

I wanted to say "no" but knew the answer was "yes." The Creator of heaven and earth gave Shellie and me three kids and was able to be trusted, no matter what.

Challenge Then Victory

Shortly afterwards we began seeing the Spirit of God move in powerful ways among the people we work with. Praise God we were able to participate in His life work by living-dead to selfish ambition and personal preference.

The Challenge

Live dead for Jesus. The question is not whether we will die but whether we will die in ways that bears much fruit.

"God, thank you for inviting me to participate in your Kingdom work. I accept your invitation to die so that I might live. Help me to die to selfish ambition so that I can find life by pursuing your will."

What are some practical ways you can start living dead today? I encourage you to respond in a personal journal or share your comments online at zachmaddox.com/faithjournal.

_____

_____

_____

_____

_____

I also encourage you to visit zachmaddox.com and select the "podcast" button for a free podcast message of this content in iTunes.

DAY 9
SPIRITUAL OLYMPIAN

"Do you not know that in a race all the runners run, but only one receives the prize? So run that you may obtain it." 1 Cor. 9:24

Running a Race as Followers of Jesus

As a former track athlete I love watching the summer Olympics. The games are defined by the dedication of athletes, the honor of representing their nation and the thrill of competition.

The amount of training is huge. Athletes plan 4 years in advance for the event. They meet with trainers, coaches, and nutritionists to become properly prepared. The athletes who compete in the 100-meter dash train 1,252 days (giving a day for rest), 5,008 hours (counting 4 hours a day). This is the equivalent of 18,028,800 seconds to run a race lasting less than 10 seconds. That is determination!

Running a Race?

In 1 Corinthians 9:24-25 Paul writes the church in Corinth and compares living for Jesus to running. Every other year Corinth would host the Isthmian games, alternating with the Olympics. The church understood competition.

Paul instructs the Corinthians to earnestly run a winning race. Like athletes you are to run the race of life with passion and enthusiasm for God and His ways.

Spiritual Disciplines

Followers of Jesus need to devote themselves to good spiritual habits.

Richard Foster's book *Celebration of Discipline: The Path to Spiritual Growth* is a great read. He writes about inward disciplines, such as prayer and Bible study.

In Foster's book he also gives attention to outward disciplines, such as service, and to corporate disciplines, like worship. [1]

Who's at the Finish Line?

You are running a race and Jesus is standing at the finish line. While the Olympic athletes will be competing for a medal, you are pursuing an eternal reward. You need to be as determined as an athlete about your spiritual training. When the race is over you will stand before Jesus and either hear, "Well done, good and faithful servant. Nice run. You studied Scripture, prayed, helped others run their race, kept your eyes focused on Me and showed love for Me. Good job!"

Or you will hear, "Depart from me, I never knew you. You didn't follow your personalized training program, didn't connect with your Trainer and had no strength and energy. You cannot be on My team. Pack your bags and leave."

The Challenge

Make good spiritual habits a matter of priority. Pursue life with purpose and live eternally for Jesus Christ.

Be intentional about spiritual training. Jesus is worth it – your eternity depends on it.

"God, give me the motivation and discipline necessary to run the race well. I want to stay focused on you and help others run the race with endurance as well."

What spiritual habits have you developed and which ones still have room for improvement? I encourage you to respond in a personal journal or share your comments online at zachmaddox.com/faithjournal.

_____

_____

_____

_____

_____

_____

_____

I encourage you to visit vimeo.com/zachmaddox/spiritual-olympian for an onsite video bible teaching captured from the ancient city of Corinth.

1 - Richard Foster. *Celebration of Discipline: The Path to Spiritual Growth.* (San Francisco: HarperSanFranciso, 1988).

.

DAY 10
A BLESSED LIFE

"I came that they may have life and have it abundantly" John 10:10

Abundance Found in Following Jesus

"I came that they may have life and have it abundantly" (John 10:10). Jesus promised an abundant life but too often a person's definition does not match what Jesus intended. Many think of abundance in cultural terms. By American standards it may be defined as a nice house, a great car, a beautiful family, and a stress-free, well-paying job. Is this what Jesus means?

Sell All That You Have

The gospel writer Mark records an incident where a rich man asked Jesus what he must do to gain eternal life. Jesus responded to obey the commandments. The man felt he was fulfilling this obligation. Jesus then said, *"You lack one thing: go, sell all that you have and give to the poor, and you will have treasure in heaven; and come, follow me" (Mark 10:21).*

This counters the thinking of abundance. Is not life

measured by possessions?

Take Up Your Cross

The gospels also record an event where Jesus was speaking to a crowd and explaining the way of salvation. *"If anyone would come after me, let him deny himself and take up his cross and follow me. For whoever would save his life will lose it, but whoever loses his life for my sake and the gospel's will save it"* (Mark 8:34-35).

Take up a cross and follow Jesus? Pick up a torturous instrument in order to experience abundance? This does not make sense. Or does it?

Redefining Abundance

Could abundance be better defined as a life with an eternal hope and with an everyday confidence? Jesus gave His followers instructions to experience abundance just before ascending to heaven.

The Greatest Commandment

Jesus commissioned His followers to *"Go therefore and make disciples of all nations, baptizing them in the name of the Father and of the Son and of the Holy Spirit, teaching them to observe all that I have commanded you. And behold, I am with you always, to the end of the age"* (Matt. 28:19-20).

The abundant life is connected to pursuing His desires. The meaning of life and a hope for the future is found as you purpose yourself to reach the nations for Him.

The rich man held back from a genuine relationship with God on account of material possessions. Jesus is more important. The abundance He talks about cannot be found unless fully devoted to Him.

Jesus said to deny yourself and carry a cross. Life will not be without struggle. Everyday challenges give the greatest opportunity to develop Christ-like character. When carrying a cross you identify with Jesus and become more like Him.

An Abundant Life

My family is experiencing "life to the full" by letting go of cultural definitions of abundance. We decided to reprioritize our lives and have faced some hardships along the way. We are richer, however, for it.

Our children are gaining a clearer worldview and learning two different languages. My wife and I have a rich sense of meaning through our work and a great hope for the future, as we experience His unfolding plan.

The Challenge

The challenge is to let go of possessions, any plans that exclude God and unrealistic expectations that keep you from experiencing the abundant life promised by Jesus.

Should hardships come Jesus will use them to shape you and to develop His nature in you.

"Jesus, I want to experience 'life to the full'. Remove my desire to create heaven on earth. Help me to develop a godly character that leads others into a relationship with you."

What holds you back from experiencing His abundance? I encourage you to respond in a personal journal or share your comments online at zachmaddox.com/faithjournal.

Faith Hope Love

_____
_____
_____
_____
_____
_____
_____
_____
_____
_____
_____
_____
_____
_____
_____
_____
_____
_____
_____

PART 2

HOPE

"I pray that God, the source of hope, will fill you completely with joy and peace because you trust in him. Then you will overflow with confident hope through the power of the Holy Spirit." Romans 15:13 - NLT

DAY 11
AN ENCOURAGING WORD

"For whatever was written in former days was written for our instruction, that through endurance and through the encouragement of the Scriptures we might have hope." Romans 15:4

Understanding the Bible

Throughout my life Scripture has encouraged and spoken to me. While living in Sudan I could identify with David crying out to God in the Psalms, *"With my voice I cry out to the Lord; with my voice I plead for mercy to the Lord. I pour out my complaint before him; I tell my trouble before him. When my spirit faints within me, you know my way!" (Psalm 142: 1-3).* Living and working in challenging locations has given me a greater understanding of his thoughts and feelings.

Christ Fulfills Scripture

Paul in Romans 15:4 encourages believers to find hope in Scripture, *"For whatever was written in former days was written for our instruction, that through endurance and through the encouragement of the Scriptures we might have hope."*

The 66 books of the Bible, one Author with 40 writers, spans 1500 years and includes history, poetry, and wisdom. The Book describes God's dramatic interaction with people.

The Old Testament prophets point to events that would occur hundreds of years later:

- Daniel 2 and 8 - the rise of Alexander the Great and the Roman Empire.

- Zechariah 12:10-13:1 - a description of the crucifixion of Christ.

- Isaiah 53 - the sufferings of Jesus.

Prophecies express the supernatural inspiration of the Bible. When people examine Scripture, taking into account the miraculous and historical elements, they discover an authenticity that points to one, perfect person - Jesus Christ.

The Authenticity of Scripture

Bruce Metzger wrote in *Chapters In The History of New Testament Textual Criticism* that the New Testament is 99.5% textually accurate. [1] No other ancient manuscript has this kind of accuracy. Over 5400 New Testament manuscripts point to its authenticity.

Our Hope is in Christ

Since Christ fulfills Scripture and promises eternal life to those who believe in Him, our confidence and hope rest in Him. As followers of Jesus hope is not found in homes, jobs, friendships, or anything offered by this world. Hope is in Christ.

The Challenge

Place your hope in the person of Jesus Christ, the fulfillment of Scripture. He is the unchanging, everlasting promise you can hold onto.

"Jesus, I place my hope in you. I know this world will pass away, but my life in you will remain. Thank you for your unchanging nature."

In what ways have you struggled to put your hope in Jesus? I encourage you to respond in a personal journal or share your comments online at zachmaddox.com/faithjournal.

_____
_____
_____
_____
_____
_____
_____
_____
_____
_____
_____
_____

1 - Bruce Metzger. *Chapters in the History of New Testament Textual Criticism.* (Grand Rapids: Wm. B. Eerdmans Publishing, 1963).

DAY 12
IN NEED OF AN ADVOCATE

"My little children, I am writing these things to you so that you may not sin. But if anyone does sin, we have an advocate with the Father, Jesus Christ the righteous." 1 John 2:1

While driving through a busy intersection in Khartoum, Sudan, my family and I were involved in a car accident. No one was hurt. Resolving the issue, however, was another matter.

Waiting For an Advocate

After spending hours at the police station, the officers determined the other vehicle had right of way. I was considered guilty of causing the collision. They required me to wait in jail for a Sudanese citizen to come and advocate my case. As a foreigner, they wanted to insure I would remain in the country and pay the repairs.

Hospitality is an important part of the Sudanese culture, so I was allowed to sit at the counter instead of behind bars. I appreciated the kind gesture and waited for my advocate.

Jesus Our Advocate

John states you have an advocate in the person of Jesus Christ, *"My little children, I am writing these things to you so that you may not sin. But if anyone does sin, we have an advocate with the Father, Jesus Christ the righteous" (1 John 2:1).*

Without Jesus you stand condemned before the holy God, unable to give a righteous plea and gain freedom from your sins. Jesus acts as an Advocate and intercedes for you. He alone has the ability to free you from sin's bondage and its consequences.

Your only hope is in Christ, the One seated at the right hand of the Judge of the whole earth, making intercession for you. *Romans 8:34, "Who is to condemn? Christ Jesus is the one who died - more than that, who was raised - who is at the right hand of God, who indeed is interceding for us."*

A Late Release

Around 11 PM, my advocate arrived at the police station and made arrangements for my release. I was thrilled not being required to stay overnight.

Jesus has come that you may be free from the darkness of sin.

The Challenge

Thank God for sending His Son Jesus to serve as your advocate. Live a life worthy of the price He paid on your behalf.

"God, thank you for sending your Son to serve as my advocate. Give me the strength to live a life worthy of Him and the price He paid on the cross."

How do you live worthy of having Jesus as your advocate? I encourage you to respond in a personal journal or share your comments online at zachmaddox.com/faithjournal.

_____

_____

_____

_____

_____

_____

_____

_____

_____

_____

_____

_____

DAY 13
TO LIVE IS CHRIST

"For to me to live is Christ" Philippians 1:21

Living as Though You do not Have Tomorrow

Our work overseas limits our ability to form concrete relationships. We make friends fast and have deep conversations. We never know when we will see each other again.

Some people quickly make an impression on you when you meet them. One summer I met such a man, Stan, a man that loves his wife, his family and his work.

Sad News

I received a message from Stan. He stated he has Stage 4 cancer. Even with chemotherapy, he only has a few months to live.

I do not know what to think about the email. I hope to catch up with him and his family, but am not sure that will be possible.

I wept for his family, prayed for healing and struggled with what this meant for his work.

Living with Conviction

Paul wrote in Phillipians 1:21-24, *"For to me to live is Christ, and to die is gain. If I am to live in the flesh, that means fruitful labor for me. Yet which I shall choose I cannot tell. I am hard pressed between the two. My desire is to depart and be with Christ, for that is far better. But to remain in the flesh is more necessary on your account."*

God's Gain is Our Loss

I know God will be pleased when Stan is in His presence. I know Stan will be blessed being in the presence of the Lord. We, however, will experience a sense of loss.

Stan has dedicated his life to and lives for Jesus. He loves his wife, his two kids, and the work God has given him.

How to Pray

The email is asking for prayer. He wants wisdom about doing chemotherapy. If the treatment will add some months to tell others about Jesus, he wants strength. If it will take away his ability to work for God, he would rather skip the treatment.

How Can Someone Make That Kind of Request?

When you spend time in the presence of Jesus, singing songs of praise, meditating on Scripture, and talking with Him, you gain a desire to serve Him and spend eternity with Him. You're hope rests in Jesus.

Stan has no regrets. His life has been well-lived. His prayer request aligns with a desire to have his remaining days filled with opportunities for Jesus.

The Challenge

Live in such a way to bring glory to God. Pursue Him and tell others about Him. Fulfill the words of Paul, "Living for Christ." Live in a way that makes your life a testimony of Jesus.

"Jesus I want to love you more. May I get lost in your presence and long for more of you each day. My life is yours."

In what ways have you "lived for Christ"? I encourage you to respond in a personal journal or share your comments online at zachmaddox.com/faithjournal.

_____

_____

_____

_____

_____

_____

_____

_____

_____

_____

_____

_____

DAY 14
DOCTORS, DIABETES, &
DEMONSTRATIONS

"Now the Lord said to Abram, 'Go from your country and your kindred and your father's house to the land that I will show you." Genesis 12:1

The Challenge of Living Overseas

My wife and I had our third child, Lucas, in the fall of 2012. Our other two children were born in the U.S. so it was interesting to figure out the process in Jerusalem. One of the challenges of living overseas is that Shellie was not been able to do as much exercise through her pregnancy which led to her developing gestational diabetes.

To help monitor the diabetes it was necessary to have regular doctor visits.

A Late Doctor

Though we live in Jerusalem the doctor worked out of

Bethlehem, about a 40-minute drive. The doctor was not at the office when we came for one of our visits. The nurse called and he arrived about 45-minutes later. He was surprised we had come. The community was planning a demonstration at 4:00 PM to show their disdain for the rising costs of gas and groceries. We were unaware of the protest and hastily finished the visit. We wanted to leave before the protest began.

The sugar level was not as we had hoped. The doctor suggested that Shellie spend the night in the hospital. This was not an option considering we had left our five-year-old son at a birthday party in Jerusalem.

Let the Demonstrations Begin

As we left the hospital there was shouting in the streets. We pulled out of the parking area and saw crowds of men blocking the way back to Jerusalem.

A Country Not Your Own

Abraham is the first recorded Biblical figure directed by God to live in a different country. *"Now the Lord said to Abram, 'Go from your country and your kindred and your father's house to the land that I will show you...I will bless you and make your name great, so that you will be a blessing'"* (Gen 12:1,2).

God designed Abraham to be a blessing to the world. This required leaving his father's household and establishing himself in another land. He obeyed God and was blessed. In turn he became a blessing.

There's Always Another Way

We could not return to Jerusalem along the same road. We thought there must be another way. Making a few quick turns down unblocked roads we found ourselves heading back to Jerusalem within 30 minutes.

Blessed to Be a Blessing

Shellie and I live with the conviction we are blessed to be a blessing to the nations. We face some interesting scenarios living in a different country. That's okay! God is greater than the challenges life offers. Our hope rests in Him. He is greater than late doctors, diabetes, and demonstrations.

The Challenge

Bless others as you go through your day. Trust God through the challenges. Sometimes a different way is possible.

"God, I put my hope in you. Thank you for being greater than any challenge life can offer. Help me to be a blessing throughout my day to those I meet."

Has God brought you through challenging moments in unique ways? I encourage you to respond in a personal journal or share your comments online at zachmaddox.com/faithjournal.

_____

_____

_____

_____

_____

_____

_____

DAY 15
A JOYFUL WORLD

Make a joyful noise to the Lord, all the earth; break forth into joyous song and sing praises!" Psalm 98:4

Christ is Coming Again

My family and I love the various holidays, especially Thanksgiving and Christmas. Whether celebrated in Chicago, Missouri, Sudan, or Jerusalem, we love decorating, reflecting on the goodness of God and giving gifts, as modeled by the Father's gift of the Son and the Magi bringing presents to Jesus.

Let Earth Receive Her King

Joy to the World, the Lord is come!

Let earth receive her King;

Let every heart prepare Him room,

And Heaven and nature sing, [1]

Prepare Him Room

God sending His Son is joyful, defeating the works of the devil and providing the way of salvation. Will the world receive the King? Will every heart prepare Him room?

Psalm 98

Issac Watts wrote the song, based on Psalm 98. Verses 4-6 read:

"Make a joyful noise to the Lord, all the earth;

break forth into joyous song and sing praises!

Sing praises to the Lord with the lyre,

with the lyre and the sound of melody!

With the trumpets and the sound of the horn

make a joyful noise before the King, the Lord!"

His Second Coming

This song is sung to celebrate the birth of Jesus in Bethlehem yet Watts wrote "Joy to the World" to celebrate His second coming, when He gives lasting peace.

A Coming Judgment

Psalm 98: 7-9 reads:

"Let the sea roar, and all that fills it;

the world and those who dwell in it!

Let the rivers clap their hands;

let the hills sing for joy together

before the Lord, for he comes

to judge the earth.

He will judge the world with righteousness,

and the peoples with equity."

Will You Be Ready?

Jesus came two centuries ago to the shouts of "Glory to God in the highest, and on earth peace among those with whom he is pleased!" He will come again for the church (His bride), and will rightfully and fairly judge the world.

The Challenge

Prepare room for Jesus in your life. Allow the Greatest King to joyfully enthrone your heart with hope. Experience the divine peace lacking in the world, coming from the Ruler of peace.

"Jesus, I crown you King of my life. I ask to be ushered into the peace only you can bring. I eagerly anticipate your second coming."

How do you express joy in your life? I encourage you to respond in a personal journal or share your comments online at zachmaddox.com/faithjournal.

_____

_____

_____

_____

_____

_____

_____

_____

_____

_____

_____

_____

_____

_____

_____

1 - Isaac Watts. *Joy to the World.* (Public Domain, 1719). First Stanza.

DAY 16
THE POWER OF PRAYER

"Save us, we pray, O Lord! O Lord, we pray, give us success!" Psalm 118:25

Godly Intervention in a Time of Need

On October 10th, 2012, a little after noon, Shellie and I welcomed our third child into the world, Lucas Ryder. A smaller bundle than the other two (weighing in at 6 lbs, 14 ounces), he is a wonderful addition to the family.

Good Son of Jerusalem

Shortly after Lucas made himself known I was following he and a nurse to the nursery where he would get more fully examined. While we were headed to the nursery, the Israeli nurse congratulated me for having a "good son of Jerusalem". In transliterated Hebrew, "waled tov Yerusalem".

When it Rains, it Pours

After we had been home a few days, we noticed that Lucas was more jaundice and that he didn't seem to be gaining weight.

Shellie also began to have some difficulties after picking up a stomach virus in the hospital. Nate came home sick from school with a fever and runny nose and our daughter, Haley, was diagnosed with an upper respiratory infection.

Calling All Saints

Shellie and I posted Facebook messages and I emailed some friends and family and asked them to pray. Within a day of that message going out, Nate and Haley seemed to be healthy, Lucas started gaining weight and losing his yellow color, and Shellie's and I's spirits were lifted.

Psalm 118:25

"Save us, we pray, O Lord! O Lord, we pray, give us success!"

We are grateful to serve a God who answers prayer. We are thankful for a worldwide body of believers who are willing to pray on our behalf. We are blessed to be a part of the kingdom of God. A kingdom of hope.

Psalm 118:28-29

"You are my God, and I will give thanks to you;

you are my God; I will extol you.

Oh give thanks to the Lord, for he is good;

for his steadfast love endures forever!"

The Challenge

If you are in need of God, seek Him in prayer. Ask others to pray with you. When you have received an answer to your prayer, give God thanks for His steadfast love.

"God, I thank you for being God. I thank you for listening to my prayers and for your steadfast love. You are good."

How has God shared His love with you lately? I encourage you to respond in a personal journal or share your comments online at zachmaddox.com/faithjournal.

_____

_____

_____

_____

_____

_____

_____

_____

_____

_____

_____

_____

_____

DAY 17
IF GOD WILLS

"Yes, a person is a fool to store up earthly wealth but not have a rich relationship with God." Luke 12:21 - NLT

Planning For a Future Not Promised

People in the Middle East have an "Inshallah" mentality. The word means, "If God wills!" The belief has several different effects on life. One relates to making future plans.

Buy Only What You Need For the Day

We recently picked up a prescription from the pharmacy. The medicine is to be taken for several months. Shellie asked the pharmacist to fill the prescription and was only given a two weeks supply. She was informed to come back in two weeks for more, not because the medicine was not in stock, but rather no one knows if it will still be needed by then.

What About Tomorrow?

Where we live people do not assume tomorrow is

guaranteed. They usually buy the groceries for a day and buy medicine needed at that moment. They rarely make preparations for the future.

What Does Jesus Think?

Luke records a parable where Jesus talks about making plans.

Luke 12:16-21

"A rich man had a fertile farm that produced fine crops. He said to himself, 'What should I do? I don't have room for all my crops.' Then he said, 'I know! I'll tear down my barns and build bigger ones. Then I'll have room enough to store all my wheat and other goods. And I'll sit back and say to myself, "My friend, you have enough stored away for years to come. Now take it easy! Eat, drink, and be merry!"' 'But God said to him, 'You fool! You will die this very night. Then who will get everything you worked for?' "Yes, a person is a fool to store up earthly wealth but not have a rich relationship with God." - NLT

Rich With God

The parable does not infer you should not plan, but does say what should get top priority – a rich relationship with God. When making plans, be sensitive to God and His will.

God's Desire

You are an eternal being meant to have a relationship with the living God. Busily pursuing wealth and menial things robs you of real hope of eternal living.

The Challenge

Live your life focused on eternity. Place God in the center of your plans. Experience true riches!

"God, give a me a rich relationship with you. Give me a desire to want more of you so that I might experience true riches, a richness that will last through eternity."

In what ways are you living for eternity? I encourage you to respond in a personal journal or share your comments online at zachmaddox.com/faithjournal.

_____
_____
_____
_____
_____
_____
_____
_____
_____
_____
_____
_____
_____

DAY 18
THE MEANING OF BETHLEHEM

"The sinless, spotless Lamb of God." (1 Pet 1:19)

Birthplace of Jesus

In 2012, we had the opportunity to celebrate Christmas Pin Jerusalem, fifteen miles from the birthplace of Jesus. Many people visit Bethlehem on Christmas Eve and Christmas Day, mostly to visit the Church of the Nativity and look at the "star-shaped" cave under the church altar where Jesus was possibly born.

Bethlehem

O holy Child of Bethlehem

Descend to us, we pray

Cast out our sin and enter in

Be born to us today

We hear the Christmas angels

The great glad tidings tell

O come to us, abide with us

Our Lord Emmanuel [1]

The Bread of Life

Bethlehem in Hebrew means "house of bread." Jesus is *"the bread of life"* and whoever receives Him will not be spiritually hungry (John 6:35). When abiding in Him you experience the greatest satisfaction in life.

The Sacrificial Lamb

Bethlehem in Arabic means "house of meat." Jesus is, *"the sinless, spotless Lamb of God" (1 Pet 1:19).* Isaiah states the Messiah *"was led like a lamb to the slaughter" (Isa 53:7).*

Cast Out Our Sin

The Child born in the place of bread and meat is the sacrificial Lamb that provides spiritual sustenance. His birth in Bethlehem points to Calvary, making a way for you to have forgiveness and fulfillment.

God With Us

Jesus, the Bread of life and sacrificial Lamb, is Emmanuel, God with us. He gives His followers hope for the future.

The Challenge

Reflect on the Christ born in Bethlehem as the Bread of life and Lamb of God. Come worship Him and experience the Lord Emmanuel.

"Jesus, thank you for coming as the bread of life and spotless, sacrificial lamb. May my life be an expression of worship to you."

How has God made Himself known in your life? I encourage you to respond in a personal journal or share your comments online at zachmaddox.com/faithjournal.

_____

_____

_____

_____

_____

_____

_____

_____

_____

_____

_____

_____

1 - Phillips Brooks. *O Little Town of Bethlehem.* (Public Domain, 1868). Fourth Stanza.

DAY 19
SEIZE THE DAY

"'Surely I am coming soon.' Amen. Come, Lord Jesus! The grace of the Lord Jesus be with all. Amen." Revelation 22:20-21

Each Day is a Gift

Nate, our kindergartner, and I walk to and from school every day. We pray about the day in the morning and he shares the best part of the day and the greatest challenge he faced on the way home. This helps him understand that each day is a gift worth remembering.

The Blessed Hope

"For the Lord himself will descend from heaven with a cry of command, with the voice of an archangel, and with the sound of the trumpet of God. And the dead in Christ will rise first. Then we who are alive, who are left, will be caught up together with them in the clouds to meet the Lord in the air, and so we will always be with the Lord" (1 Thessalonians 4:16-17).

Eternity on Your Mind

At one time the church liberally sang choruses referencing the second coming of Christ, such as "The King is Coming; Soon and Very Soon; and We Shall See the King."

Carpe Diem

The result was a sense of urgency to make the most of every moment, knowing you either move people closer to heaven or hell by the way you live. Living with the imminent return of Christ creates an urgency to tell others about Him and seize each day for Jesus.

Always With the Lord

In the toils of life there is a longing for more of Him, a longing not fully actualized until He returns and the church is caught up to Him in the clouds. Eternity is your final rest, remaining forever in His presence. What a day that will be!

The Return of the King

The Bible closes with *Revelation 22:20-21, "'Surely I am coming soon.' Amen. Come, Lord Jesus! The grace of the Lord Jesus be with all. Amen."*

Our blessed hope is the return of Jesus Christ.

A Final Act

These verses confess that answers to life's problems do not rest in human ability. The answer comes in the return of Him who brings lasting peace.

Redemptive history remains incomplete until Christ returns.

The Challenge

Make the most of each day, live expecting the return of

Christ and do not miss a moment telling others about Him. "Amen. Come Lord Jesus!"

"Come Lord Jesus. I long to be with you in eternity. But until you come, help me to consider each day a gift, an opportunity to tell others about your goodness."

How can you begin to live each day with intentionality? I encourage you to respond in a personal journal or share your comments online at zachmaddox.com/faithjournal.

_____

_____

_____

_____

_____

_____

_____

_____

_____

_____

_____

PART 3

LOVE

"Now we see things imperfectly, like puzzling reflections in a mirror, but then we will see everything with perfect clarity. All that I know now is partial and incomplete, but then I will know everything completely, just as God now knows me completely. Three things will last forever - faith, hope, and love - and the greatest of these is love." 1 Corinthians 13:12 –

NLT

DAY 20
BLESSED ARE THE PEACEMAKERS

"God blesses those who work for peace, for they will be called the children of God." (Matthew 5:9) - NLT

Rockets From Gaza

In the fall of 2012, Israel and the Gaza strip exchanged rockets. Having a rocket fired toward Jerusalem forced me to think about those facing a great number of rocket attacks. Sitting in the dimly lit bedroom of my children one evening, waiting for them to drift off to sleep, I wondered what it was like for families going to bed in Gaza City and Ashkelon. They regularly face threats of rockets and bombs.

The Gulf War - Operation Desert Storm

While attending middle-school I watched televised footage of American troops working to expel Iraqi soldiers from Kuwait, easily disconnecting the bombing and loss of life taking place an ocean away.

Bomb Shelters in Ashkelon

We live within 50 miles of Gaza and, yet, it is hard to imagine the daily threat and stress of rockets fired 8 to10 miles away. Ashkelon deals with missiles fired from Gaza and the Iron Dome missile defense system shooting them down. Most of the rockets are destroyed but some pass through the defenses.

Funds were raised for bomb shelters in Ashkelon because of the continual threat. They were trying to find peace of mind in a challenging location.

Tragedy in Gaza

Israel responded to attacks by bombing sites within Gaza. Innocent people now live among the wreckage. A BBC correspondent stated, "A mother in her wrecked home is scurrying around collecting her daughter's dolls, dusting them off."

By the time the firing stopped, 133 Palestinians and 6 Israeli's were dead. Where will they spend eternity?

Praying For the Peace of Jerusalem

Matthew 5:9 records Jesus saying, *"God blesses those who work for peace, for they will be called the children of God."* - NLT

Psalm 122:6 gives instruction to, *"Pray for the peace of Jerusalem!"* Many churches tell me they regularly pray for peace. What kind of peace are they praying for?

Palestinians Keeping Jesus From Returning

I was invited to a dinner in Jerusalem and met a Palestinian Christian whose family has always lived in Israel. He visited a church in the United States and was warmly welcomed as "a guest from Israel." When people greeted him at the end of the service, a man shook his hand and said, "I've longed to shake the hand of a Jew from Israel." The guest informed him he loves the Jewish people but was a Palestinian Christian. The church member pulled his hand away, turned and walked away.

These kinds of experiences cause Palestinian believers to ask, "What's wrong with me; what's wrong with my Christianity; am I keeping Jesus from coming again?"

The Church Keeping Jesus From Coming

The only thing keeping Jesus from coming is the church fulfilling her mission, seeing people from every tribe and nation recognize Jesus as Lord. *Matthew 24:14, "And this gospel of the kingdom will be proclaimed throughout the whole world as a testimony to all nations, and then the end will come."*

Pray For the Peace of Jerusalem

If praying for the peace of Jerusalem, pray for the Prince of Peace to infiltrate the hearts of all Jerusalem's inhabitants. Pray for the secular Israeli, the orthodox Jew, the religious Armenian, and the hard-line Muslim to experience hope and love in Jesus.

May they experience His peace, even when sirens warn of incoming missiles! Hope is in the King of Kings and in His eternal confidence, not on being spared from tragedy.

The Challenge

Embrace the commands of Jesus to love God and love people - all people.

Be willing to go and tell others about Him, teaching them about God and the eternal destiny found in Christ. Pray for peace and proclaim His message around the world.

"Jesus, thank you for true, inner peace. May I see others as you see them. Help me to find ways of promoting your peace in the world. "

What are some practical ways you can love, go, teach? I encourage you to respond in a personal journal or share your comments online at zachmaddox.com/faithjournal.

_____

_____

_____

_____

_____

_____

_____

_____

_____

_____

_____

_____

_____

_____

_____

DAY 21
PRISON GUARD OR WALMART GREETER

"And he arose and came to his father. But while he was still a long way off, his father saw him and felt compassion, and ran and embraced him and kissed him." Luke 15:20

How Are We to Handle the Message of Jesus?

My kids are suckers for stickers. Our 2-year old daughter can get high fevers. After being poked and prodded during a visit to the doctor she loudly exclaimed, "Where's my sticker?" The doctor laughed and happily gave her a sheet of them.

Whenever we visit a Walmart, we are warmly greeted and my two kids usually are offered yellow, smiley-face stickers. The greeters seem to have an endless supply of them and are happy to give them away.

Which One Are You?

On the flip side are prison guards. Their job is very different from a Walmart greeter. They hold the keys to security doors and keep people in and others out.

Bob Goff (@bobgoff) tweeted, "Some of Jesus' guards turned into followers; His followers don't need to turn into guards. Everyone's invited." [1]

Compassionate or Angry

His tweet reminded me of a message I heard on the Prodigal Son. The speaker gave a vivid example of two different gatekeepers. When the prodigal son turned down the road to come back to his father's house the gospel of Luke records, *"And he arose and came to his father. But while he was still a long way off, his father saw him and felt compassion, and ran and embraced him and kissed him"(Luke 15:20).*

The prodigal's brother is also part of the story. He was angry about his brother's celebrated return. Had he not been in the field when his brother returned, would he have guarded the doorway to the house? Would he have held the keys to the door, keeping those he wanted inside and keeping others out?

What Kind of a Believer Are You?

Are you a Walmart greeter, happily portraying love to everyone you meet? Do you show love and compassion to those considered undeserving? Or would you rather be a guard, holding keys to a life-changing message and choosing who gets to hear?

The Challenge

Jesus invites everyone. The Good News is for "whosoever will." Let the love of Jesus permeate every fiber of your being so that others want what you have, membership in God's family.

"God forgive me if I have kept others from knowing you. May I welcome people into your kingdom by the way I speak and interact with them. Let your love flow through me."

In what ways have you been attracted to Jesus by the way you witnessed other people living? How have you been handling the message of Jesus? I encourage you to respond in a personal journal or share your comments online at zachmaddox.com/faithjournal.

_____

_____

_____

_____

_____

_____

_____

_____

_____

_____

_____

_____

_____

1 - Bob Goff. Used by permission of @*bobgoff*. (Posted on Twitter, June 24,   2012).

DAY 22
HUNGRY FOR GOD

"As a deer pants for flowing streams, so pants my soul for you, O God. My
soul thirsts for God, for the living God." Psalm 42:1-2

Desiring More

There has been stirring within me a desire to experience
more of God. The book of Acts continually states the early
believers were "full of faith" and "full of the Spirit." I deeply want
these qualities and, when the need arises, to be used in supernatural
ways.

The Pursuit of God

God has laid out the way to a deeper relationship with Him:
Be filled with the Holy Spirit, read and meditate on Scripture, pray
and fast, and be part of a faith community (the church).

Feasting on the Lord

When fasting, take extra time to feast on the Lord. Scripture
reading, prayer, and singing are acts of feasting while abstaining

from food.

A Prayer Walk

Wanting to dedicate a day to prayer, I hiked a trail at En Gedi near the Dead Sea. It is an oasis in the desert with streams, palm trees, and caves, located about 18 miles south of where Jesus is thought to have spent 40 days in the wilderness. The place was one of the locations where David hid from Saul.

Experiencing God

Before leaving for En Gedi, Shellie and I prayed. I sensed more of God while hiking because I came prepared for more of Him. Scripture promises, *"Draw near to God, and he will draw near to you"* *(James 4:8)*.

The God not defined by boundary or location, resides in those calling Him Lord.

Increasing and Decreasing

The hike became a prayer journey, asking for me and my family to be full of faith and full of His Spirit. I sang songs that express hunger for His presence.

One of the comments of John the Baptist, who ministered just north of En Gedi, became a Scripture prayer, *"He must become greater and greater, and I must become less and less"* *(John 3:30)* - NLT.

Expecting to Encounter God

Pastors often request people come to church prepared. Just showing up for a gathering is not enough. Believers should walk with God all weeklong and come ready for an encounter with Him.

To love God means having a vibrant on-going relationship with Him, a relationship not confined to church gatherings but lived-out throughout the week.

The Challenge

Passionately pursue the living God. Expect Him to fill you with the Holy Spirit. Regularly read the Bible, pray, and fast. A.W. Tozer writes in *The Pursuit of God*, "We pursue God because, and only because, He has first put an urge within us that spurs us to the pursuit...The impulse to pursue God originates with God, but the outworking of that impulse is our following hard after Him." [1]

God is pursuing you, are you pursuing Him?

"God, I want more of you. I want to be full of faith and full of the Spirit. May You become greater as I become less."

How have you pursued a deeper relationship with God? I encourage you to respond in a personal journal or share your comments online at zachmaddox.com/faithjournal.

_____

_____

_____

_____

_____

_____

_____

1 - A.W. Tozer. *The Pursuit of God*. (Public Domain: Christian Publications, Inc., 1948). 10-11.

DAY 23
ABIDING IN THE VINE

"Abide in me, and I in you. As the branch cannot bear fruit by itself, unless it abides in the vine, neither can you, unless you abide in me." John 15:4

Bearing Fruit in Jesus

Genesis 1 gives the assignment to be productive. *"Be fruitful and multiply and fill the earth and subdue it" (v. 28).* Adam and Eve were to be fruitful, have fruitful children, and extend fruitfulness throughout creation. The Old Testament continues the metaphor of fruit to describe people who love, serve and live for God.

Bearing Fruit

New Testament believers are also told to bear fruit, which requires abiding in Jesus.

John 15:1-5

"I am the true vine, and my Father is the vinedresser. Every branch in me that does not bear fruit he takes away, and every branch that does bear fruit he prunes, that it may bear more fruit. Already you are clean because of the

word that I have spoken to you. Abide in me, and I in you. As the branch cannot bear fruit by itself, unless it abides in the vine, neither can you, unless you abide in me. I am the vine; you are the branches. Whoever abides in me and I in him, he it is that bears much fruit, for apart from me you can do nothing."

The True Vine

Jesus' departure was coming closer and His disciples would no longer be with Him physically. In one of His farewell discourses they are told about a new way to be with Him, a fruit-bearing kind of connection.

Jesus states, *"I am the true vine."* The quality of fruit depends on the vine that produces it. When a person is attached to Jesus, their fruit will be of superior quality.

The Vinedresser

The relationship between the believer and God is similar to the vine and the vinedresser. He cultivates and tends to the vine, seeking to produce a maximum yield.

God desires for to you experience an abundant yield of fruit; to develop fully the fruit of love, joy, peace, patience, kindness, goodness, faithfulness, and self-control. (Galatians 5: 22-23)

The Vinedresser, God, is seeking to clear obstacles that hinder the life-giving flow of His Spirit through the vine, rendering it useless; things such as pride, selfishness, materialism, and unwholesome thoughts. If something makes you inactive or unproductive, the Lord addresses it out of love.

Abiding in Jesus

Abiding is the necessary prerequisite of fruitfulness. Continued production depends on constant union with the Source of good fruit.

"Apart from me you can do nothing." Apart from Jesus the meaning of life cannot be found. Apart from Jesus there is no hope for the future. Apart from Jesus nothing of significance is accomplished.

I Can Do All Things

Counter this with the words of Paul, *"I can do all things through him who strengthens me"* (Phil 4:13).

For your life to be significant and filled with purpose you must abide in Him.

The Challenge

Display your love of God by daily being with Jesus! Abide means "to remain." Remain in His presence, meditate on His Word, linger in prayer and worship, and ponder on the thoughts of Christ.

"God I choose to express my love for you by remaining in your presence. I recognize that apart from you I can nothing of lasting significance. Help me to take more time daily to abide in you."

How do you take time to abide in Jesus? I encourage you to respond in a personal journal or share your comments online at zachmaddox.com/faithjournal.

_____

_____

_____

_____

_____

_____

_____

_____

_____

_____

_____

_____

_____

I also encourage you to visit zachmaddox.com and select the "podcast" button for a free podcast message of this content in iTunes. The podcast shares practical ways to abide in Jesus.

DAY 24
PRAYING SCRIPTURE

"This kind cannot be driven out by anything but prayer." Mark 9:29

Become More God-possessed

Jesus was asked to heal a demon-possessed boy. The father had already asked the disciples to deliver him but they were unable. After Jesus cast out the demon the disciples asked Him why they failed. *"He said to them, 'This kind cannot be driven out by anything but prayer'" (Mark 9:29).* The boy was more demon-possessed than the disciples were God-possessed. Becoming God-possessed is through prayer.

Praying Scripture

One form of praying involves Scripture. As you read the Bible personalize verses with prayer.

The Armor of God (Ephesians 6:10-18)

Scripture states you are to "put on" God's spiritual armor. By prayer clothe yourself and get dressed in His armor.

• The helmet of salvation – "Guard my mind by the

atonement of Calvary – my attitudes, ambitions, and motives. Cover my thoughts with salvation."

• The breastplate of righteousness – "Guard my heart with Your righteousness. May my passions and desires be clothed in decency and help me to do what is right"

• The belt of truth – "Surround my life with truth. Keep me from faltering or stumbling in times of struggle and conflict."

• The feet shod with the gospel of peace – "May the Good News determine my path, having each step saturated with peace."

• The shield of faith (a movable protection) – "May faith shield me from every slanderous accusation, wherever they might come. May these cunning flaming missiles fall harmlessly to the ground."

• The sword of the Spirit – "May the Word of God be effectively applied in every situation I encounter."

Developing Fruit (Galatians 5:22-25)

At conversion the fruit of the Spirit is implanted in the heart: *"Love, joy, peace, patience, kindness, goodness, faithfulness, gentleness, and self-control."* At first the fruit appears as a small seed and needs growth. You should regularly ask for the Spirit's fruit to ripen and be more fully seen in your life.

The fruit (singular) of the Spirit (Gal 5:22) is contrasted with the desires (plural) of the sinful nature (Gal 5:19). Sinful desires leave a life fragmented and broken but the fruit of the Spirit can unify and restore wholeness.

Supernatural Gifts (1 Corinthians 12:7-11)

The fruit of the Spirit reflects Jesus natural attributes. Paul also writes about His supernatural attributes. Supernatural gifts are available and should be manifested, as needs arise:

- Three manifest supernatural insight – word of wisdom, word of knowledge, and the discernment of spirits.

- Three manifest supernatural intervention - faith, healing, and miracles.

- Three manifest supernatural inspiration - tongues, interpretation of tongues, and prophecy.

Pray for God to use you to manifest His supernatural nature. Stay sensitive to the leading of the Holy Spirit.

The Challenge

There are many Bible verses waiting for you to personalize. Scripture praying enhances spiritual advancement. Pray God's word over your family, as well.

Regularly pray:

- To be clothed with His armor.

- For the fruit of the Spirit to ripen.

- For His gifts to be manifested through you.

An unbelieving generation needs to see Jesus in your everyday conduct, both naturally and supernaturally. Be willing to enter into spiritual conflict for their destiny. Love through prayer!

"God, help me to put on your full armor. I need the fruit of the Spirit to ripen in my life. I desire to be used in supernatural ways, as needs arise. Ready me for your work."

What scriptures have you prayed over your life? I encourage you to respond in a personal journal or share your comments online at zachmaddox.com/faithjournal.

_____

_____

_____

_____

_____

_____

_____

_____

_____

_____

_____

_____

_____

_____

DAY 25
PRAYING THE DISCIPLES PRAYER

"Our Father in heaven, hallowed be your name. Your kingdom come, your will be done, on earth as it is in heaven." Matthew 6:9,10

The Prayer

"Our Father in heaven, hallowed be your name. Your kingdom come, your will be done, on earth as it is in heaven. Give us this day our daily bread, and forgive us our debts, as we also have forgiven our debtors. And lead us not into temptation, but deliver us from evil." Matt. 6:9-13

Complementing Sides

Various people have written of ways to apply the Lord's Prayer. One way is to divide the content in two, a God side and human side.

Realigning with God

The God side includes four parts:

- *"Our Father"* - praying unselfishly for Him to lovingly rule your request.

- *"Your Name"* - praying for His character to be contained within your prayer.

- *"Your Kingdom"* - praying for His kingdom to be the focus of every desire.

- *"Your Will"* - praying for His will to be manifested in every appeal.

Realizing Results

The human side also contains four parts:

- *"Give us"* - praying for personal needs, without the needs of others being jeopardized.

- *"Forgive us"* - praying for forgiveness, with a determination to forgive others.

- *"Lead us"* - praying for His leading, knowing the pathway will be free of temptation.

- *"Deliver us"* - should there be failure to follow His lead, ask for an escape from evil.

The Heartbeat of Prayer

Prayer involves realignment with results following. The process of realignment and results is ongoing. To the measure you realign to God, you experience an equal measure of results. The more you adjust to Him, more effects follow.

Unselfish Prayers

Praying unselfishly is also an integral part of prayer. Our Father, give us, forgive us, and deliver us are rooted in community. The more you attach yourself to Jesus and those who follow Him, the more relevant is your prayer. Pray with others in mind.

The Challenge

Pray to realign with God and for His kingdom to advance by the fulfillment of His will. If the eternal side is right, temporal needs are also met.

Pursue Him and forgive the transgressions of others! God will supply every need.

"God, I desire to pray your will. May I usher in your kingdom by the way I live. Please forgive me for falling short of your expectations. I want to be more like you."

How is God leading you? I encourage you to respond in a personal journal or share your comments online at zachmaddox.com/faithjournal.

_____

_____

_____

_____

_____

_____

_____

_____

_____

_____

_____

DAY 26
LOVING PEOPLE WHILE HATING TOLERANCE

"Love the Lord your God with all your heart and with all your soul and all your mind ...(and) love your neighbor as yourself." Matthew 22:37, 39

Our culture strongly endorses tolerance. Is it healthy for the church to embrace this trait? Is tolerance equal to love?

"Kind People Go to Heaven!"

While visiting a cafe' in Jerusalem I found a tip jar with a note attached that stated, "Tip, because kind people go to heaven." The pervading thought of "kind people go to heaven" is deeply ingrained in many cultures. Not offending others has become top priority today. Tolerance seems to reflect kindness. This has led many to think tolerance is love.

Love God, Love People

Jesus said the greatest commandments are to, *"Love the Lord your God with all your heart and with all your soul and all your mind ...(and) love your neighbor as yourself"* (Matthew 22:37, 39).

We align with God and ask the Spirit's fruit to increase in our life – love, joy, peace, patience, kindness, goodness, faithfulness, and self-control.

We experience more of His transforming power and naturally start wanting to tell others about Jesus. We love neighbors and even enemies. We want them to experience life to the fullest.

An Eternal Concern

To not express concern for a person's eternal welfare is not love but passivity.

Love does not include blind tolerance for unwholesome lifestyles that separate people from God.

Bringing a Sword

The message of salvation can bring division. Jesus states, *"Do not think that I have come to bring peace to the earth. I have not come to bring peace, but a sword"* (Matt. 10:34).

Social norms support people with unbiased tolerance for any lifestyle. Expect conflict when upholding biblical values.

Love and Division

When lovingly talking with others about God, the message may not be appreciated. This should not change your God-given burden to see them rescued from eternal separation with the Creator. Oswald Chambers encourages, "Never be diplomatic and careful with the treasure God gives you." [1]

Defining Love

Tolerance is easy, love is hard. As someone who follows the One bringing meaning to life and hope for the future, choose love.

Real love leads people to a relationship with God. We have a treasure to give and tolerance will not save people from hell.

Please Excuse My Intolerance

If you do not follow Jesus, please excuse me for refusing to passively walk through life, ignoring a lifestyle not exhibiting a meaningful relationship with God.

I cannot idly stand by and watch you live a life displeasing to God, keeping you separate from Him.

Excuse my intolerance but accept my love and concern for your eternal destiny. *John 3:16, "For God so loved the world, that he gave his only Son, that whoever believes in him should not perish but have eternal life."*

The Challenge

Genuinely love! Be bold! Share your faith! Do not let tolerance stand in the way of telling others what God will do for them, about the forgiveness and freedom experienced when following Jesus.

"God, I love you and my neighbor. Help me to find ways to show others your love, even when it's hard. May those not in relationship with you find the forgiveness and freedom they long for."

What are some ways you can express love to your neighbor? I encourage you to respond in a personal journal or share your comments online at zachmaddox.com/faithjournal.

_____

_____

_____

_____

_____

_____

_____

_____

_____

_____

_____

_____

_____

1 - Taken from *My Utmost for His Highest* by Oswald Chambers, edited by James Reimann, © 1992 by Oswald Chambers Publications Assn., Ltd., and used by permission of Discovery House Publishers, Grand Rapids MI 49501. All rights reserved.

DAY 27
STORMING THE GATES OF HELL

"The reason the Son of God appeared was to destroy the works of the devil." 1 John 3:8

Bringing Love, Justice, and Peace to the World

What is our role as the church? To discover this we need to look at Jesus and His work on earth. 1 John 3:8 states: *"The reason the Son of God appeared was to destroy the works of the devil."*

The cross is victory over the powers holding people in bondage; sin, death, and the devil. As God's emissaries, believers are called and empowered to continue the work Jesus began with his life, death and resurrection.

Jesus desires to use you to build His church and advance His kingdom. Matthew 16 helps you to better understand your role.

Matthew 16:15-18

He (Jesus) said to them, "But who do you say that I am?" Simon Peter replied, "You are the Christ, the Son of the living God." And Jesus answered him, "Blessed are you, Simon Bar-Jonah! For flesh and blood has not revealed this to you, but my Father who is in heaven. And I tell you, you are Peter, and on this rock I will build my church, and the gates of hell shall not prevail against it."

City of False Gods

Jesus travels with His disciples 20 miles north of Galilee to the district of Caesarea Philippi. In this area is a rocky hillside where shrines dedicated to the god of Pan, Echo, and Hermes existed. Next to these shrines is a large cave where a powerful stream once flowed, called the "gates of hell".

The worshipers of Pan would perform human sacrifices in the cave and cast the remains into a natural abyss at the back of the cave.

The Living God

In this area where other god's required human sacrifice, Peter confesses Jesus to be "the Son of the living God." God brings life, not death. Jesus promised in John 10:10, *"I came that they may have life and have it abundantly."*

An Advancing Kingdom

In this passage Jesus is saying, "The church will overcome these lesser gods - the god of Pan, Echo, and Hermes. Other gods focus on self, materialism, pride, fame, sex, power and bring death. I will build my church over these things and the gates of hell shall not prevail against my advancing kingdom."

Storming the Gates of Hell

We advance the kingdom by charging the gates of hell, as inaugurated by God's reign of love, justice, and peace. Where there is despair, bring hope. Where there is unbelief, bring faith. Where there is hatred, bring love. Where there is sickness, offer healing.

We are to be walking, talking, representatives of Jesus to the world.

Committed to the Church

Connect to a community of faith. You cannot effectively advance the kingdom of God on your own. Believers working together with a common goal make it happen.

We need one another. Paul refers to the church as the Body of Christ, with everyone having an important function. You need the church and the church needs you.

Promised Victory

When we work together what does Jesus say will happen? *"They shall not prevail against us!"* The keys of the kingdom have been given to us.

Victory has been promised. We simply need to be willing to advance on the gates of hell.

The Challenge

Commit yourself to the task of storming the gates of hell until His imminent return. Be intentional to turn people to Jesus at home and work by displaying His love, justice, and peace to the world.

"Jesus, I commit to the Church and it's mission. May I display your love, justice, and peace to the world."

What are some ways that you can storm the gates of hell? I encourage you to respond in a personal journal or share your comments online at zachmaddox.com/faithjournal.

_____

_____

_____

_____

_____

_____

_____

_____

_____

_____

_____

_____

I also encourage you to visit zachmaddox.com and select the "podcast" button for a free podcast message of this content in iTunes.

DAY 28
FAITH, HOPE, AND LOVE ABIDE

"So now faith, hope, and love abide, these three; but the greatest of these is love." (1 Cor. 13:13)

An Authentic Faith

Jerusalem is a city of many faiths: Christianity, Islam, Judaism, and Orthodoxy. This creates an interesting environment to live and work. As part of a Jesus-centered community, people who believe differently frequently wonder about us. Some have remarked, "You are from different parts of the United States, yet there is a spirit that unites your group. You seem to really love each other."

An authentic display of God's love is attractive to the world.

Love the Greatest

The virtues of faith, hope, and love embrace life in the Spirit and the return of Christ. In some ways faith and hope give more attention to the individual while love addresses the wider community. People are saved by faith and hope but the kingdom of

God depends on love. Love unites.

Faith

Believers have faith in God and trust Him to forgive and accept them through Christ. They cannot visibly see Him yet trust in His goodness and grace.

In eternity the trust in God that began in this life continues. Faith becomes sight.

Hope

Believers also have hope for a future guaranteed through Jesus. By His resurrection they are future-oriented people. They know the present is on its way out. They are on a journey to a place in the presence of God, seeing Him face to face.

In eternity hope becomes realized.

Love

Love is the greatest because love unites believers with God. *"In this is love, not that we have loved God but that he loved us and sent his Son to be the propitiation for our sins...We love because he first loved us"* (1 John 4:10,19).

Through God's love followers of Jesus are able to love one another. By loving one another they display God's love to the world. *"By this all people will know that you are my disciples, if you have love for one another"* (John 13:35).

In eternity love becomes fully actualized.

The Challenge

Have great faith in God, profound hope in the future, and a deep love for Jesus and the church. May the love you show others reflect Christ to the world!

"God, I thank you for faith, hope, and love. I can't wait for my faith to become sight, my hope to be realized, and my love to become complete. But until that day, help me to display your love to the world and draw others to faith and hope in you."

In what ways can you grow your faith, hope, and love? I encourage you to respond in a personal journal or share your comments online at zachmaddox.com/faithjournal.

_____
_____
_____
_____
_____
_____
_____
_____
_____
_____
_____
_____
_____
_____

A BIBLICAL THEOLOGY OF THE HOLY LAND

Living in Jerusalem, we are often asked about the land and people. I decided to write a biblical perspective of the Holy Land. I am also part of a project giving a concise-visual representation of the subject. As an added value, the content is added to this devotional. May it challenge and encourage you to fulfill Jesus' command to love God, love people and make disciples of all peoples. The Apostle John reveals the conclusion:

"After this I saw a vast crowd, too great to count, from every nation and tribe and people and language, standing in front of the throne and before the Lamb. They were clothed in white robes and held palm branches in their hands. And they were shouting with a great roar, "Salvation comes from our God who sits on the throne and from the Lamb!"

And all the angels were standing around the throne and around the elders and the four living beings. And they fell before the throne with their faces to the ground and worshiped God. They sang, "Amen! Blessing and glory and wisdom and thanksgiving and honor and power and strength belong to our God forever and ever! Amen." Revelation 7:9-12 - NLT

HOLY LAND

"When Joshua was near the town of Jericho, he looked up and saw a man standing in front of him with sword in hand. Joshua went up to him and demanded, 'Are you friend or foe?'

'Neither one,' he replied. 'I am the commander of the Lord's army.'" Joshua 5:13,14 - NLT

God Dwelling with His People

What is the significance of the place called the Holy Land, the parcel of land located on the eastern shores of the Mediterranean? What makes a land holy? The answers are found in the narrative of Scripture.

The Bible as Narrative

The Bible is written as a dramatic narrative, containing four parts:

- *Exposition* - Genesis 1-2

- *Complication* - Genesis 3

- *Climax* - Revelation 20

- *Denouement* - Revelation 21-22

Genesis 1 and 2 (creation) covers the exposition, the part of the story describing the original state of affairs. Genesis 3 (the rebellion of man) lays out the complication, the part of the story disrupting the status quo. The main portion of the Bible develops the story, stemming from the complication (disobedience to God). Revelation 20 presents the climax, the defeat of evil. Finally, in Revelation 21 and 22 is the denouement, the New Heavens and New Earth. The denouement becomes the new status quo, after the complication is resolved.

Man and woman start in the Garden of Eden in full communion with God with both the tree of life and tree of knowledge of good and evil. Mankind finishes in the New Heavens and New Earth in full communion with God with the tree of life, having experienced the fruit of the tree of knowledge of good and evil and evil being defeated. Revelation 22:2 states, *"on either side of the river, the tree of life with its twelve kinds of fruit...The leaves of the tree were for the healing of the nations."*

What does this have to do with the Holy Land?

The Holy Land and Older Covenant

The Holy Land is part of the creation story, with the Garden of Eden being the original location. The garden is the first place "flowing with milk and honey," where Adam rules as a kingly priest and serves God in a garden-temple. According to Sam Brelo, "Adam, as God's son, lived in Eden and therefore enjoyed the rest of God, symbolizing God's sovereign rule."[1] Adam is given the command to multiply and subdue the earth. The whole earth was to enjoy the glorious presence of God.

Adam failed to obey and was removed from the sanctity of the garden-temple. The first Holy Land became lost to mankind. As history unfolds the human race continues to rebel and attempts to become unified in a manmade sanctuary on the plains of Babel.

God separates the nations.

Finally, the Lord sees promise in a man called Abraham and extends to him two promises: a kingly people and a kingdom land. A Holy Land is promised to Abraham as, *"to the land that I will show you" (Genesis 12:1).*

God gave the Garden of Eden as an inheritance to Adam and gave Canaan, a type of the Garden of Eden, as an inheritance to Israel. Adam's enjoyment of God's presence and the first Holy Land were based upon obedience. Obedience is the same condition upon which Israel may enjoy God's presence and live in the second Holy Land.

Leviticus 18:25 declares, *"Because the entire land has become defiled, I am punishing the people who live there. I will cause the land to vomit them out" - NLT.* Similar passages are located in Deuteronomy 28:63, Joshua 23:16, and throughout the Old Testament.

In Ezekiel 37-48 Israel's redemption is described as a return to the Holy Land, as well as the reestablishment of the Davidic kingship and Levitical priesthood. Israel's salvation meant dwelling with God around His Temple in a divine inheritance, the Holy Land.

Israel staying in the Holy Land with God was guaranteed through continued cleansing and holiness, as portrayed in the Law of Moses. Without atonement by various sacrifices and worship, Israel was subject to expulsion.

The Holy Land and New Covenant

The writer of Hebrews states Jesus fulfills the sacrificial practices of the Law by His supreme sacrifice. The Levitical priesthood also became fulfilled by His priesthood (Hebrews 7:18-19). Therefore, the Temple and Holy Land become better understood in Christ.

The writer of Hebrews also shares that although Joshua

brought Israel into the Holy Land, he did not give them the rest of God (Heb 4:8). Sam Brelo gives insight, "the reason for this is that the Temple in the Holy Land is not the true dwelling place of God; it is only a 'pattern' of heavenly realities (Heb 8:1-5)."[2]

Jewish belief is based on the Torah, Temple, and Territory. Jesus on several occasions encountered people desiring an earthly kingdom. They hoped He was *the one to redeem Israel" (Luke 24:21)*. They considered Israel's redemption being the restoration of the nation and the cleansing of the Holy Land, more than mankind's salvation.

Jesus brought fulfillment in a different way. Through the Incarnation the Lord would dwell among His people (John 1:14). Jesus would be the divine Temple, the place where God is experienced and worshiped.

Jesus also became the Holy Land. He states in John 15 of being the "true vine." Connection with God would no longer be attached to a tract of land. Being part of the Holy Land would now require being grafted into Jesus. Jesus declared being in the Father's presence was no longer territorial but spiritual. (John 14:1-11)

The Holy Land, where God dwells with His people, is the unquestioned inheritance of Abraham's descendants. The Apostle Paul states the inheritance includes Jews and Gentiles: *"Know then that it is those of faith who are the sons of Abraham" (Galatians 3:7)*. Being sons of Abraham is by faith and Jesus, God's Son, is the centrality of faith. Those in Christ have become children with divine inheritance. The place of God's dwelling is gained through faith (Galatians 3:26, 29).

The quintessence of the book of Revelation is the New Heaven and New Earth, culminating in chapters 21 and 22. The vision of the New Heaven and New Earth is the climax, not only of the Bible but of the whole salvation story. The final vision is essentially a re-creation of the Garden of Eden, the garden-temple of God. The prophetic revelation brings believers to the hope of the final Holy Land, where the purpose of the Garden of Eden and the land of Canaan is fulfilled. With the creation of the New Heaven and New Earth, God establishes a new sanctuary where He and the children of inheritance dwell forever.

Defining the Holy Land

The Holy Land and its purpose is one of the important threads running through Scripture. God's story begins and ends with Him living with His creation in a secure, peaceful and sanctified space. In the redemption story God calls Abraham out of Ur, giving Canaan to him and his descendants as an inheritance. The Holy Land belongs to God and He calls out the elect, providing a place where He can restfully dwell with them. Occupying the Holy Land by Abraham's descendants was conditional upon love and obedience to God.

In the fullness of time, God sends His Son to reveal His glory and to tabernacle among His creation. The Holy Land receives its fulfillment in Jesus. By abiding in Christ through love and obedience believers find peace and rest and are a sanctified temple of worship. This is experienced by the indwelling of His Spirit and is fully experienced in the New Heaven and New Earth, the place where the children of inheritance live unimpeded with God in the final and everlasting Holy Land.

God dwelling with His children in a holy dwelling place centers in Christ. The Good News to both Jews and Arabs in the Middle East is the same; God desires to live with His children eternally. Anyone can become His child and live with Him through Jesus. The Holy Land and its purpose are inseparably linked to having faith in Christ. Outside of Christ, there is no divine inheritance.

Whose Side Are You On?

Those who follow Jesus are to follow in His footsteps and fulfill His command to love God and people - all people. Those with faith in Christ are to be world-changers, showing equal value to all peoples and nations.

Joshua 5:13-14 gives guidance, *"When Joshua was near the town of Jericho, he looked up and saw a man standing in front of him with sword in hand. Joshua went up to him and demanded, 'Are you friend or foe?'*

'Neither one,' he replied. 'I am the commander of the Lord's army.'" Joshua 5:13,14 - NLT

When asked, "Whose side are you on, Arab or Jew?" respond, "Neither, I'm for all peoples and nations, to the glory of God!"

Revelation 7:9, *"After this I looked, and behold, a great multitude that no one could number, from every nation, from all tribes and peoples and languages, standing before the throne and before the Lamb."*

I encourage you to visit vimeo.com/zachmaddox/holy-land to view *Holy Land* **– a concise, visual representation of this subject.**

For a more in-depth study read, *God Dwelling with His Children in Paradise: A Biblical Theology of the Holy Land* **by Sam Brelo. Available on Amazon.**

1 - Sam Brelo. *God Dwelling with His Children in Paradise: A Biblical Theology of the Holy Land.* (CreateSpace, 2012). 6.

2 - Sam Brelo. *God Dwelling with His Children in Paradise: A Biblical Theology of the Holy Land.* (CreateSpace, 2012). 68.

ABOUT THE AUTHOR

Zach is a cross-cultural educator, speaker, and writer with experience teaching in Florida and the Chicago area. Zach oversaw a school in Khartoum, Sudan and currently directs a school in Jerusalem, Israel.

Zach and his family lived in Khartoum for two years and now reside in East Jerusalem. Through their work in education Zach and his family encourage students and families to live according to the teachings of Jesus and promote positive change in their communities and nations.

Zach maintains a weekly blog at zachmaddox.com, produces a weekly blogcast on iTunes, publishes video bible teachings at vimeo.com/zachmaddox and posts daily inspiration on Twitter @zachmaddox.

Zach and Shellie, along with their three children, long to see Jesus unveiled in the hearts and minds of people around the world.

A FINAL PRAYER

"May God bless you with discomfort at easy answers, half truths, and superficial relationships so that you may live deep within your heart.

"May God bless you with anger at injustice, oppression, and exploitation of people so that you may work for justice, freedom, and peace.

"May God bless you with tears to shed for those who suffer pain, rejection, hunger, and war so that you may reach out your hand to comfort them and turn their pain into joy.

"And may God bless you with enough foolishness to believe that you can make a difference in the world, so that you can do what others claim cannot be done to bring justice and kindness to all our children and the poor."

-A Franciscan Benediction

21 DAYS OF QUIET CONTEMPLATION

Unveil Me

experiencing freedom by
removing veils of deception

Shellie Maddox

FOREWORD BY DARLA RAKES

www.ingramcontent.com/pod-product-compliance
Lightning Source LLC
Chambersburg PA
CBHW020548030426
42337CB00013B/1017